Mr Tilly's
Bake it yourself Book

Tatterdemalion Blue

First published by **Tatterdemalion** Blue in 2017

Words © Noreen Leighton 2017

Illustrations © Lorna Wilson 2017

Noreen Leighton and Lorna Wilson have asserted their right
to be identified as the author and the illustrator of this work
in accordance with the Copyright, Design and Patents Act 1988

All rights reserved. No part of this publication may be reproduced,
stored in a retrieval system, or transmitted in any form or by any means,
electronic, mechanical, photocopying, recording or otherwise,
without the prior permission of the copyright owner

A CIP catalogue record for this book is available from the British Library

Cover design and layout by **Tatterdemalion** Blue

ISBN 978-0-9933114-6-8

Tatterdemalion Blue

21 Underwood Cottages

Cambusbarron

Stirling FK7 9PA

www.tatterdemalionblue.com

Mr Tilly's
Bake it yourself Book

Written by Noreen Leighton
Illustrated by Lorna Wilson
Recipes by Nora Gilfillan

In loving memory of Noreen Leighton
1957 - 2017

... a beautiful, generous, talented, bright shining soul ...
Author of the Mr Tilly books

To the ones we love.. you know who you are :)

Special Thanks to the Tilly Tearoom
in Tillicoultry & Dunblane - Bonnie Scotland

~ . ~

The inspirational home of Mr Tilly

The Recipes in this Book

have been imagined and written by Noreen,
created and tested by Nora,
and lovingly drawn by Lorna.

And now they can be baked and eaten by you!

This could be the beginning of a love of baking
that will last all of your life.

So, get your apron on,
wash your hands and let's get started xxx

Recipes

Spring
Mabel's Easter Surprise Creme Egg Cupcakes — 3
Bridget's Jammy Tarts — 7
Mrs Irvine's Loving Lemon Drizzle Cake — 10
Mrs Gilmore's Gluten Free Marshmallow Crispy Cakes — 13

Summer
Faerie Cakes — 19
Rossa's Blueberry Muffins — 23
Keely's Swirly Pink Cupcakes — 26
Mungo's Hearty Carrot Cake Delight — 28
Nora's Hummingbird Cake — 32

Autumn
PC Bryce's Digger Biscuits — 39
Pete the Goldfish's Scary Ginger Biscuits — 42
Heather's Tablet — 45
Archie Russell's Treacle Buns — 48
Daisy's Pumpkin Biscuits — 52

Winter
Bridget's Exceptional Christmas Clusters — 57
Sarah's Star Biscuits — 60
Mr Patel's Orange and Cranberry Muffins — 64
Alison's Mum's Chocolate Brownies — 67

Have fun ...

Spring

The squirrels and rabbits are wide awake
The birds have begun to sing.
The sun feels warm, no need for a coat,
I think it must be Spring.

I see the buds upon the trees
New life in everything.
There are lambs and calves out in the fields,
I think it must be Spring.

Let's have a go at Jammy Tarts
And start to learn to bake.
Spring is a new beginning
So let's start with Cream Egg Cupcakes.

There are Easter Bunny Biscuits
And Lemon Drizzle too.
They will smell and taste delicious
And all be made by YOU.

Recipes

Mabel's Easter Surprise Creme Egg Cupcakes

Bridget's Jammy Tarts

Mrs Irvine's Loving Lemon Drizzle Cake

Mrs Gilmore's Gluten Free Marshmallow Crispy Cakes

Mabel's Easter Surprise Creme Egg Cupcakes

What you need in the kitchen

WEIGHING SCALES
WOODEN SPOON
(or electric mixer if you have one)
TEASPOON
TABLESPOON   FORK
ONE LARGE MIXING BOWL SIEVE
TWO SMALLER BOWLS   WIRE RACK
MUFFIN TIN   12 PAPER CUPCAKE CASES

Ingredients (what's in it!)

for the cupcakes
125g caster sugar
125g margarine
2 eggs
100g self-raising flour
Pinch of bicarbonate of soda
25g cocoa powder
1 teaspoon vanilla essence
2 tablespoons milk
12 creme eggs
12 mini creme eggs (to decorate)

for the vanilla frosting
125g butter
250g sieved icing sugar
2 teaspoons vanilla essence
2 tablespoons milk

Here we go …

1. Put the yummy creme eggs into your freezer.
2. Ask a Grown-Up to put the oven on 180 °C (160 for a fan oven) Gas Mark 4.
3. Put the paper cases into the muffin tin.
4. Crack the eggs into a small bowl and whisk them up with your fork. Set aside.
5. Weigh out your flour and cocoa powder into a second small bowl along with that pinch of bicarbonate of soda. Set aside.
6. Now put 125g of caster sugar and 125g of margarine into the bigger bowl and beat them together with your wooden spoon until light, fluffy and soft.
7. Add some egg and mix with your spoon, then some flour. Then add the vanilla essence. Keep stirring and mixing egg and flour, one after the other.
8. When you have mixed in all the flour and egg, stir in the 2 tablespoons of milk and stir stir again.
9. Dollop one small spoonful of the mixture into each muffin case. Take the creme eggs out of the freezer and put one into each muffin case, followed by another small dollop of cake mixture.
10. Don't over fill the cases as the cupcakes will rise. Just fill enough so that the top of the creme egg is just showing. Bake in the oven for 15 minutes.
11. Take the cupcakes out of the oven with the help of your Grown-Up.
12. Let them cool in the tin for a few minutes then place them onto the wire rack … REMEMBER …

You cannot decorate them until they are COMPLETELY COOL!

To make the vanilla frosting

1. In your bigger bowl which you have washed up and using your wooden spoon beat up the butter until it is pale and creamy looking.
2. Weigh out your icing sugar. Put it through a sieve so that there are no lumps and slowly mix it into the creamy butter.
3. Add the vanilla essence and milk and keep stirring. It will start to look soft and creamy.
4. Using your teaspoon, swirl some of this creamy mixture on top of each cupcake.
5. Cut the mini creme eggs in half and place on top of each cupcake for decoration.

WOW YUM!!!

Mr Tilly's Tips

Mabel's Easter Surprise Creme Egg Cupcakes

What is a pinch?
When you see a pinch of bicarbonate of soda or a pinch of salt in a recipe it just means what you can pick up between your thumb and your finger.

Tablespoon?
This big metal spoon is the size of two pudding spoons so if you don't have one in your kitchen worry not.
Just use a pudding spoon.

1 tablespoon = 2 pudding spoons

Beating the butter or the eggs?
This really isn't as bad as it sounds!
It just means mixing something backwards
and forwards to make it softer or to stir it all up.

You need strong wrists to beat
so if it gets too much for you pass it over
to a Grown-Up. If they are not strong enough
there is always the food mixer machine!

Bridget's Jammy Tarts

What you need in the kitchen

A ROLLING PIN
COOKIE CUTTERS
(a bigger one for the base
and perhaps a star or something like it for the top)
A FORK
A TEASPOON
A CAKE TIN FOR MAKING WEE CAKES OR TARTS
A WIRE RACK

Ingredients (what's in it!)

A packet of readymade shortcrust pastry
A little flour for dusting
A little butter for greasing
Jam (Pick your favourite flavour)
Icing sugar for yet more dusting!

This one is easy so let's get started ...

1. Ask a Grown-Up to set the oven to 200 °C (180 for a fan oven) Gas Mark 6.
2. Put a dod of butter onto some greaseproof paper and grease the cake tin.
3. Sprinkle (or dust) some flour onto the table or where it is you want to roll out your pastry. Remember to also put some flour on the rolling pin too so it doesn't stick.
   WHOOPS!!!
4. Roll out the pastry to the thickness of a one pound coin.
5. Using your larger pastry cutter press onto the pastry and cut out 12 circles.
6. Prick the circles with your fork and put them into the greased cake tin.
7. Using your teaspoon, place one spoonful of jam into the centre of each tart.
8. Roll out your leftover pastry. Don't forget to flour the table and rolling pin if they need it and cut out your twelve stars or hearts.
9. Place the stars or hearts on top of the jam.
10. Bake in the oven for 12-15 minutes. When they are ready they will be golden and smell delicious.
11. Let the tarts cool a little then carefully take them out of the tin. A Grown-Up is useful here.
12. Put them on a wire rack.
13. Once the tarts have cooled, sprinkle (or dust) them with icing sugar and EAT.

Mr Tilly's Tips

Bridget's Jammy Tarts

Cake tin - Muffin tin?
Cake tins usually look like this ...

Muffin tins are deeper and look like this ...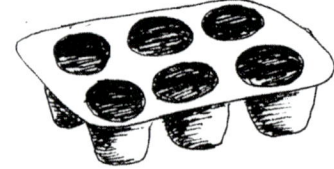

Dusting with flour?
I thought dusting was something Bridget did around the ornaments in our flat above the teashop. She has a yellow duster and one feathery thing that she likes to tickle me with!

But when you are baking, 'dusting' means sprinkling over lightly. Dusting with flour or dusting with icing sugar.

Dust that rolling pin!
When you are rolling out pastry don't forget to dust (sprinkle lightly) the surface underneath first so it doesn't stick. Also, dust the rolling pin so it doesn't stick to that too.
LOTS OF DUSTING means NO STICKING.

Mrs Irvine's Loving Lemon Drizzle Cake

What you need in the kitchen

WEIGHING SCALES
1KG (2LB) LOAF TIN
BIG MIXING BOWL
SAUCEPAN
WOODEN SPOON
TABLESPOON
SIEVE
KNIFE

Ingredients (what's in it!)

275g margarine for baking
225g caster sugar
5 eggs
275g plain flour
2 tablespoons baking powder

For the drizzle crust

4 tablespoons lemon juice
1 tablespoon golden syrup
2 tablespoons granulated sugar
Dod of butter for greasing

Ooh! This cake is scrumptious let's make it ...

1. Ask a Grown-Up to set the oven to 180 °C (160 for a fan oven) Gas Mark 4.
2. Put a dod of butter onto some greaseproof paper and grease the bread tin.
3. Weigh the butter and sugar. Put them into the mixing bowl and using your wooden spoon, beat them together until they are light and creamy.
4. Beat in all those eggs. Have a cracking time.
5. Weigh and sieve the flour and fold this into the mixture along with the baking powder and salt.
6. Spoon the mixture into the bread tin, levelling off the top.
7. Bake the cake for 1 hour and fifteen minutes. You will know it is ready if you put a knife in and it comes out clean. (This is a job for a Grown-Up).
8. Remove the cake from the oven and leaving the cake in the tin stab the knife right through in several places.
9. In the saucepan warm up the lemon juice, then add the syrup and sugar. Straight away spoon this all over the cake. The syrup will soak through and the sugar crystals will stay on the top.
10. Put the cake in the fridge to chill and when you are ready, remove it from the tin and slice it up to share.

NOW THAT'S ENOUGH TO MAKE MY TAIL WAG.

Mr Tilly's Tips

Mrs Irvine's Loving Lemon Drizzle Cake

Folding

Well I have heard of folding paper. I have even heard of folding clothes but what does it mean when you are baking?

Bridget says it means mixing something in gently and quickly without stirring things up too much. A bit like folding the mixture over what you are adding to it. Cosy.

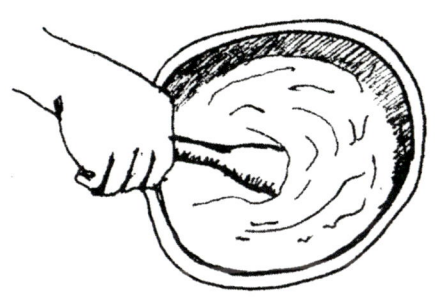

A Dod's a dod!

You may have noticed that I keep asking for a dod of butter. This is a good Scottish word meaning a wee bit or a small amount. We speak a whole other language up here but we don't want to confuse anyone.

Mrs Gilmore's Gluten Free Marshmallow Crispy Cakes

What you need in the kitchen

WEIGHING SCALES
DEEP BAKING TRAY
BRUSH (for oiling)
SAUCEPAN
TABLESPOON
WOODEN SPOON
PAPER CASES

Ingredients (what's in it!)

250g toffees
50g butter
3 tablespoons milk
115g marshmallows
175g gluten free Rice Krispies
Vegetable oil for brushing!

You don't need the oven for this one ...

1. Lightly brush a deep baking tray (a roasting tin would be okay) with a little vegetable oil.
2. Weigh out the toffees and butter and along with the milk put them into the saucepan.
3. Heat gently and stir with a wooden spoon until the toffees have melted.
4. Weigh out the marshmallows and Rice Krispies and stir them into the melted toffee.
5. Spoon the mixture into the baking tray and level off.
6. Put the tray into the fridge to cool and set.
7. When it is cool and hard, cut into squares.
8. Put the squares into paper cases.

PERFECT FOR SHARING ... WOOF WOOF

Mr Tilly's Tips

Mrs Gilmore's Gluten Free Marshmallow Crispy Cakes

Brushing the tin?

There are lots of types of brushes. Great big ones on the end of a long stick that are fun to chase, fat stubby ones that come with their own dustpan. Brushes to glue with, brushes to paint the walls with, special brushes for Peter the Artist's paintings.

Bridget even has a brush for my coat but the less said about that the better. But when it comes to baking, it is called a pastry brush. It's a useful thing for brushing oil or egg or milk over things. Check it out.

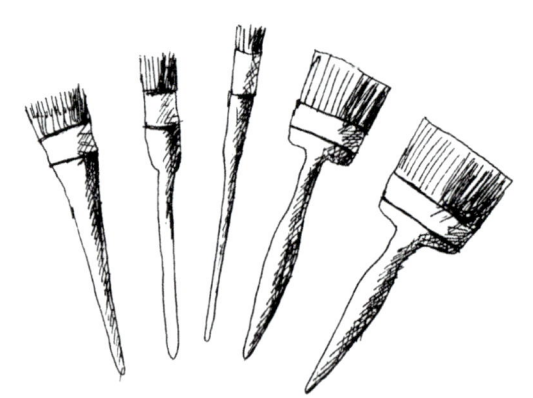

Paper cases

You can buy all sorts of different paper cases in the shops or online. All sizes and all colours. You can even find wee boxes to put your baking in and give as presents.

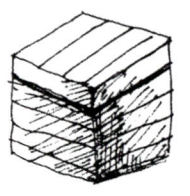
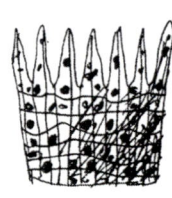

Summer

The faeries love the Summer
When fruits and flowers delight.
The vegetables are growing
And the days are long and bright.

The teashop door is open
To allow a little breeze.
I smell cut grass and barbecues
As I scamper midst leafy trees.

It is a magic time of year
When the hills are all aglow.
When faeries dance by the river's edge
And great fish swim below.

Let's see what the faeries would like us to make
To create a glorious tea.
Muffins and cupcakes for picnics
In the shade of a fine old tree.

Recipes

Faerie Cakes

Rossa's Blueberry Muffins

Keely's Swirly Pink Cupcakes

Mungo's Hearty Carrot Cake Delight

Nora's Hummingbird Cake

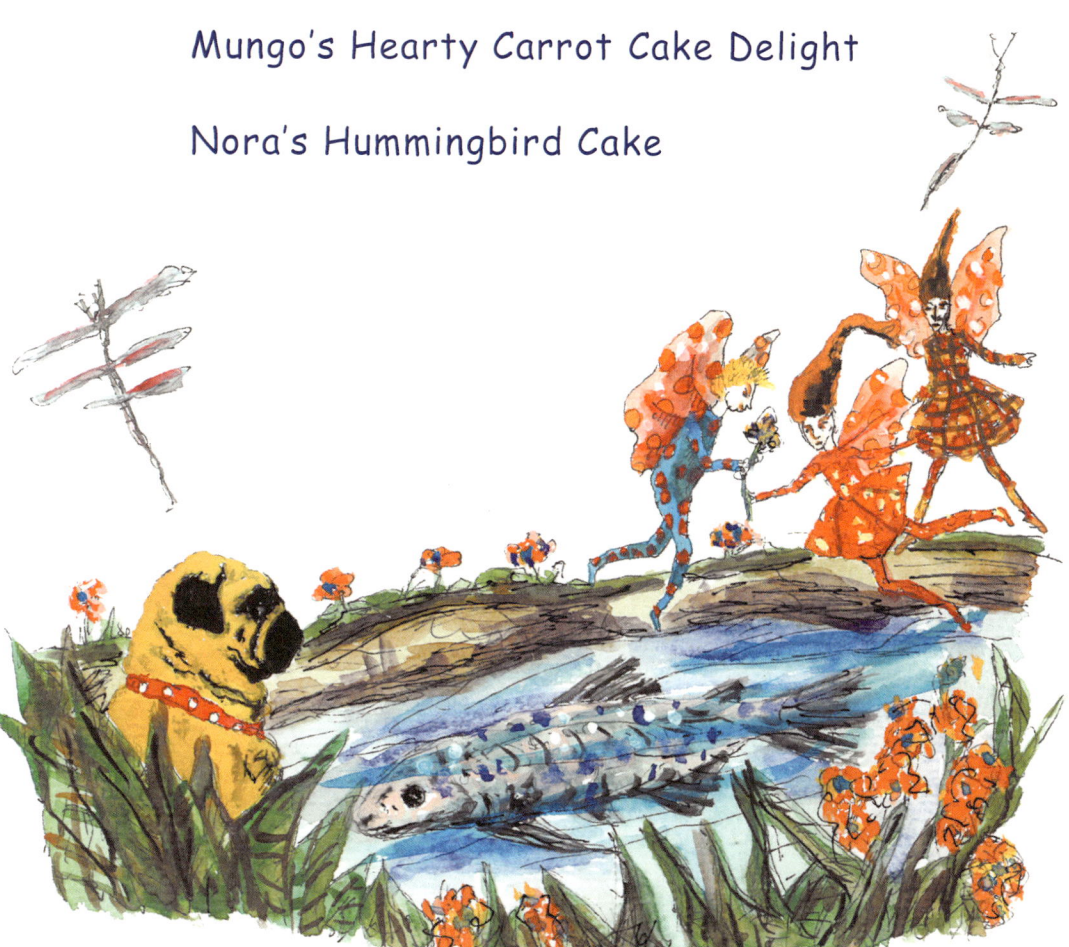

Faerie Cakes

What you need in the kitchen

MUFFIN TIN
LARGE MIXING BOWL
WEIGHING SCALES
SMALLER MIXING BOWL
TEASPOON
KNIFE

12 PAPER MUFFIN CASES
WOODEN SPOON
SIEVE
MEASURING JUG
WIRE RACK
ELECTRIC HAND MIXER

Ingredients (what's in it!)

110g unsalted butter at room temperature
225g caster sugar
150g self raising flour
120ml semi skimmed milk

2 large eggs
125g plain flour
1 teaspoon vanilla extract

for the vanilla icing

110g unsalted butter
1 teaspoon vanilla extract
60ml semi skimmed milk (at room temperature)
500g of sifted icing sugar

No guessing why these are a Faerie's favourite ...

1. Ask a Grown-Up to set the oven (or preheat it) for you to 160°C/ Gas Mark 3.
2. Put the paper cases into the muffin tin.
3. Weigh out your butter and sugar.
4. Put them into the large mixing bowl.
5. Using the wooden spoon (or a mixer if there is a Grown-Up helping) cream the butter and sugar together until they are smooth and pale in colour.
6. Break in the eggs one at a time, mixing for a few minutes after each has gone in.
7. Weigh out the flours and using the sieve sift them together into the smaller mixing bowl.
8. Measure out the milk into the measuring jug and add the vanilla extract to it.
9. Add about a third of the flours to the creamed mixture and beat well.
10. Pour in about a third of the milk and beat again.
11. Repeat these steps until all the flour and all the milk has been mixed in.
12. Using the teaspoon and your clean pinkie carefully spoon the mixture into the muffin cases until each is about two thirds full.
13. Ask a Grown-Up to pop the muffin tray into the heated oven and bake for 25 minutes until slightly raised and golden brown. Whilst the cakes are baking do your washing up.
14. Cool the muffins on the wire rack.
    Whilst they are cooling you can make the vanilla icing ...

15. Weigh out the 110g of butter and put it into the large mixing bowl along with the 60ml of milk and vanilla extract.
16. Weigh out the 500g of icing sugar then using your sieve sift half of it into mixing bowl.
17. Ask a Grown-Up to mix it all together using an electric hand mixer.
18. Add the rest of the icing sugar a little at a time and mix until the icing is smooth and creamy. YUM!
19. Now it is time to decorate your cakes ... Cut a slice off the top of each cake and cut the slice in half.
20. Spread a layer of the vanilla icing over the cut cakes.
21. Take the two halves of the sliced cake and stick the middle edges down into the middle of the cakes to make faerie wings.
22. Dust with icing sugar.

NOW THESE ARE MAGICAL CAKES!

Mr Tilly's Tips

Faerie Cakes

Room temperature?

When you see that butter or milk should be kept at room temperature, it means, TAKE IT OUT OF THE FRIDGE FOR A WHILE so butter is softer and milk not cold.

Semi skimmed milk?

Milk is either WHOLE, SEMI SKIMMED, OR SKIMMED. This tells us how much FAT they have in them. You can tell the difference by the colour of their top.

WHOLE = BLUE TOP
SEMI SKIMMED = GREEN TOP
SKIMMED = RED TOP

Pinkie?

Your pinkie is your wee finger, furthest away from your thumb!

Rossa's Blueberry Muffins

What you need in the kitchen

LARGE MIXING BOWL
CUP (normal teacup)
SIEVE
TEASPOON
LARGE METAL SPOON
MUFFIN TIN

SMALLER MIXING BOWL
WEIGHING SCALES
GRATER
MEASURING JUG
12 MUFFIN PAPER CASES
WIRE RACK

Ingredients (what's in it!)

180g plain flour
Three quarters cup of sunflower oil
60g caster sugar
1 teaspoon vanilla essence
1 teaspoon grated lemon rind
1 and a half cups of fresh blueberries
Quarter of a teaspoon of salt
2 eggs

If you are going on a picnic these are the best ...

1. Ask a Grown-Up to set the oven to 200 °C/Gas Mark 6.
2. Place the muffin cases in the muffin tin.
3. Weigh and sieve the flour and sugar and put into the large mixing bowl.
4. Add the baking powder and salt.
5. Crack and whisk the eggs in the smaller bowl and then add the oil, vanilla, milk and grated lemon rind.
6. Make a well in the centre of the flour and sugar in the big bowl.
7. Pour the eggs etc. into the well.
8. Use the metal spoon to mix it all up but don't over do it.
9. Carefully fold in the blueberries.
10. Spoon the mixture into the muffin cases being careful not to over fill them so that there is space for the cakes to rise.
11. Bake for 20 - 25 minutes until the tops spring back when you touch them lightly.
12. Leave them in the tin for a few minutes to cool a wee bit then pop them onto a wire cooling rack.

ACTUALLY I THINK THESE ARE BEST WHEN THEY ARE STILL A LITTLE WARM SO THEY ARE GOBBLED UP QUICKLY!

Mr Tilly's Tips

Rossa's Blueberry Muffins

Grated lemon rind?

When it comes to a lemon or an orange or even a lime, the outer layer is called the rind and the juice inside is called the pith.

To get the rind we rub the fruit against a grater (a bit like grating cheese.)

To get the pith we squash the fruit onto one of these ...

Juicy.

Make a well?
When the recipe says 'make a well' it means scoop a hole out in the middle.

Filling the cases?
Remember that your cakes are going to rise up when they are baking so don't overfill the cases. Give them room to GROW.

Keely's Swirly Pink Cupcakes

Now to make these gorgeous cupcakes see the recipe for ...

Faerie Cakes

1. Once you have mixed up your cake mixture divide it into two bowls and add a few drops of PINK FOOD COLOURING to just ONE of the bowls and mix well.
2. Taking your teaspoon, spoon a small amount of the plain mixture to one side of each paper muffin case and then a spoon of the pink mixture.
3. Then just stir round once so that the mixture has a marbled effect.
4. After baking, make the vanilla icing as described for Faerie Cakes but add a few drops of PINK COLOURING to turn it a glorious PINK.
5. Now instead of making the wings take the pink coloured icing and SWIRL IT on top of each cake.

WOWZER!!!

Mr Tilly's Tips

Keely's Swirly Pink Cupcakes

How to do the swirly bit!

Mungo's Hearty Carrot Cake Delight

What you need in the kitchen

18CM ROUND LOOSE BOTTOMED CAKE TIN
WEIGHING SCALES
SMALL MIXING BOWL   LARGE MIXING BOWL
GRATER   GREASEPROOF PAPER
KNIFE   FORK
TEASPOON   WOODEN SPOON
WIRE RACK   PENCIL AND SCISSORS

Ingredients (what's in it!)

225g self-raising flour
150ml sunflower oil
2 teaspoons baking powder
175g cream cheese
115g chopped dates
175g icing sugar
2 small ripe bananas mashed
225g grated carrots
Dod of butter for greasing
2 eggs

This is Mungo's absolute favourite and it's healthy too ... YIPPEE

1. Ask a Grown-Up to set the oven to 180 °C/Gas Mark 4
2. Using a dod of butter on a small piece of greaseproof paper grease the cake tin.
3. Put the base of the tin onto a fresh piece of greaseproof paper and draw around it with your pencil.
4. Cut out the circle and put it in the bottom of the cake tin.
5. Weigh out the flour and sugar and put them into the large mixing bowl.
6. Add the baking powder and dates and stir it all together with your wooden spoon.
7. Ask a Grown-Up to grate the carrots and then using your hands give the grated carrot a good squeeze to get out the liquid.
8. Add the squeezed carrot to the mixture in the big bowl.
9. Mash up the bananas and add them to the mixture too. Set this bowl to one side.
10. In the smaller mixing bowl crack in the eggs and pour in the oil and beat them together with a fork.
11. Now pour the beaten eggs into the flour etc. in the bigger mixing bowl and beat it all together with your wooden spoon.
12. Spoon this lovely mixture into the cake tin and level off the top with a knife.
13. Cook for 1 to $1\frac{1}{2}$ hours until a Grown-Up puts in the knife and it comes out clean.

14. Remove the cake from the tin very carefully, (ask a Grown-Up to help you) and put it on the wire rack to COOL DOWN.
15. Wash and dry your small mixing bowl, fork and knife.
16. Weigh out your icing sugar and beat it and the cream cheese together in the bowl with your fork.
17. When the icing is smooth and thick, spread it over the cooled down carrot cake with the knife.

HOT CARROTS WHAT A COOK!

Mr Tilly's Tips

Mungo's Hearty Carrot Cake Delight

Lining the tin?

1. Take a sheet of greaseproof paper.
2. Pop your cake tin on top.
3. Using a pencil carefully draw around the tin.
4. Cut out the shape.
5. Place it in the bottom of the tin
6. It should be a perfect fit.
   If it is too big cut it a little bit more.

Cool that cake?
Before you decorate COOL - that is the RULE.

Nora's Hummingbird Cake

What you need in the kitchen

TWO 7 INCH SANDWICH TINS
GREASEPROOF PAPER
SIEVE
KNIFE
LARGE SPOON
TEASPOON
ELECTRIC HAND MIXER
PENCIL AND SCISSORS

FOOD MIXER
WEIGHING SCALES
WIRE RACK
FORK
LARGE MIXING BOWL
MEASURING JUG
TIN OPENER
PALETTE KNIFE

Ingredients (what's in it!)

300g caster sugar
225ml vegetable cooking oil
1 teaspoon of cinnamon
1 small tin of crushed pineapple
Dod of butter for greasing tins

3 small eggs
300g self raising flour
1 big banana
75g chopped pecan nuts

for the vanilla icing

110g unsalted butter
1 teaspoon vanilla extract

60ml semi skimmed milk
500g icing sugar

I feel a song coming on ...

1. Ask a Grown-Up to preheat the oven to 180 °C/Gas Mark 4
2. Take one of the cake tins and put it on top of a sheet of greaseproof paper.
3. Using your pencil draw around it. Then repeat again.
4. Cut out the two circles with scissors.
5. Take a piece of the left over greaseproof paper and using a dod of butter grease the base of both tins.
6. Place the circles in and grease them a little too.
7. Weigh out the caster sugar and put into the food mixer along with the eggs.
8. Ask a Grown-Up to help you mix them up until they are thick and creamy.
9. Measure out the oil in the measuring jug and whilst the mixer is slowly turning add it to the mixture until thoroughly mixed.
10. Turn off the mixer while you weigh out the flour then sift it into the mixture along with a teaspoon of cinnamon. Mix it in for a moment.
11. Turn off the mixer while you mash the banana with a fork and open the tin of pineapple.
12. Add these plus the chopped nuts to the mixture and give it a good mix.
13. Pour or spoon the mixture into the cake tins so that they look as though they hold the same amount.
14. Ask a Grown-Up to put them in the oven and bake for half an hour. Or you can do the knife test - *SEE MY TIPS*.

15. Turn out the cakes onto a wire rack to cool and peel off the greaseproof paper.
16. Now make the vanilla icing. Measure out the butter on the scales and the milk in the measuring jug and put them into the large mixing bowl. Add the vanilla extract too.
17. Weigh out the icing sugar and put half of it into the mixture.
18. Using the hand held mixer mix everything up for several minutes until smooth.
19. Bit by bit add the rest of the icing sugar and mix until smooth and creamy.
20. Once the cakes have cooled, using a palette knife (or an ordinary knife will do), spread some of the icing on one of the cakes and sandwich the cakes together.
21. Spread the remainder on top of the cake, then make swirly designs with a fork.

CHAMPION CAKE I SAY.

Mr Tilly's Tips

Nora's Hummingbird Cake

What is the knife test?

Sometimes it isn't easy telling if your cake is cooked so we need to do the knife test. This should be done by a GROWN-UP because the oven will be very HOT.

Open the oven and gently put a knife into the middle of the cake. If it comes out clean your cake is cooked, but if it has gooey mixture on it the cake needs longer in the oven.

Turning out a cake?

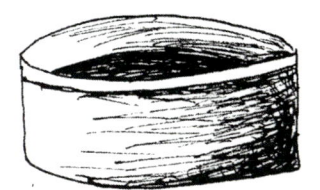

If you have greased the tins well then this part is easy. Place the wire rack over the top of the cake and flip it over so that the rack is underneath. Using the blunt end of a knife gently tap the cake tin until you feel the cake come away onto the rack. Lift off the tin and **THERE IS YOUR PERFECT CAKE**.

The secret is plenty of greasing.

A sandwich cake?

In the tea shop a favourite is a Victoria Sandwich Cake which is two sponge cakes with jam in between them. So when it says sandwich cakes together it simply means put them together with jam or icing in the middle ... **OOH YES!!!**

Autumn

The trees have all got orange leaves
That float in the air and fall.
I love it when Bridget kicks them up
While I try to catch them all.

Everything is ripened
And the geese are flying over.
The swallows have gone, hedgehog's asleep
And the days are feeling cooler.

Let's make some scary biscuits
For the night when we go guising.
The treacle buns are such a treat
With games like apple bobbing.

Make the tea and light the fire
And pass the biscuit tin.
Or share some creamy tablet chunks
As the dark night draws us in.

Recipes

PC Bryce's Digger Biscuits

Pete the Goldfish's Scary Ginger Biscuits

Heather's Tablet

Archie Russell's Treacle Buns

Daisy's Pumpkin Biscuits

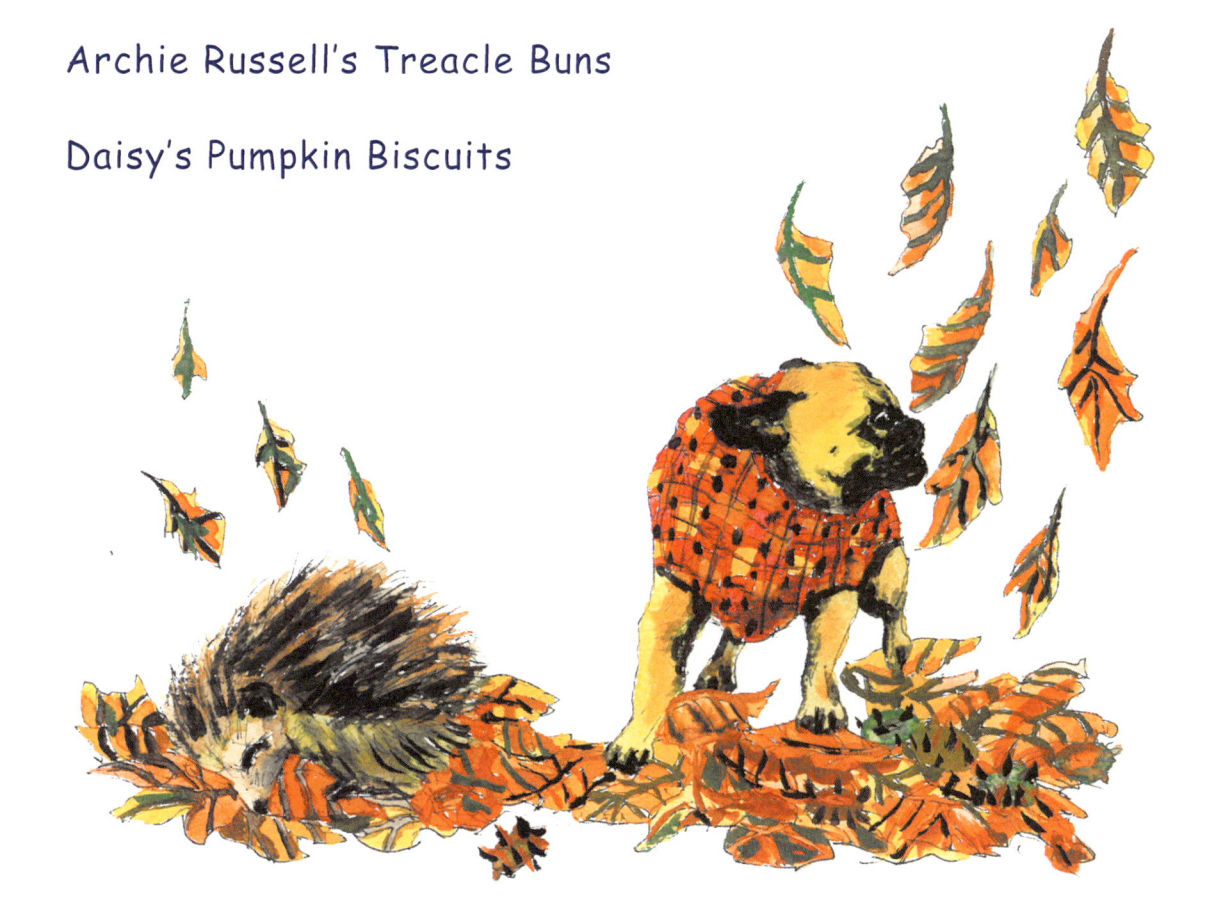

PC Bryce's Digger Biscuits

What you need in the kitchen

WEIGHING SCALES
TEASPOON
SIEVE
FORK

WIRE RACK
TABLESPOON
2 BAKING TRAYS
FLAT KNIFE OR SPATULA

Ingredients (what's in it!)

175g golden caster sugar
125g self raising flour
70g porridge oats
40g desiccated coconut
140g unsalted softened butter
1 tablespoon black treacle
1 teaspoon bicarbonate of soda
Dod of butter for greasing

These are so quick and easy ...

1. Ask a Grown-Up to set the oven to 180 °C/Gas Mark 4.
2. Using a dod of butter on a little greaseproof paper lightly grease the two trays.
3. Place ALL the ingredients into the mixing bowl and mix together well using your fork.
4. Once it is all mixed together take small pieces of the dough (this is what your mixture is now called) and roll into balls the size of walnuts.

DID SOMEBODY SAY BALL? WHERE'S MINE?

5. Place these balls well apart on the baking trays.
6. Flatten them a little using the prongs of the fork.
7. Bake for 15 minutes or until golden brown. They will feel soft when you take them out of the oven but will firm up nicely once they cool down.
8. Leave them on the tray for a few minutes then carefully lift them onto the cooling rack with a flat knife or spatula.

WATCH OUT HERE COMES PC BRYCE
AND IT TAKES A LOT OF BISCUITS TO FILL THOSE BOOTS!

Mr Tilly's Tips

PC Bryce's Digger Biscuits

Make sure your butter or margarine is soft soft soft!!!

You may be very strong and a wiz with a wooden spoon but even the strongest man in the village or indeed your Grown-Up's electric food mixer would struggle if the butter isn't soft.

Take it out of the fridge at least an hour before you start baking.

Pete the Goldfish's Scary Ginger Biscuits

What you need in the kitchen

WEIGHING SCALES
BAKING TRAY
TABLESPOON
ROLLING PIN
WIRE RACK

LARGE MIXING BOWL
WOODEN SPOON
TEASPOON
BISCUIT CUTTERS
SMALL MIXING BOWL

Ingredients (what's in it!)

115g soft brown sugar
115g soft margarine
Pinch of salt
4 drops of vanilla essence
175g wheat grain flour
1 tablespoon cocoa powder
2 teaspoons ground ginger
2-4 tablespoons hot water
225g icing sugar
A little milk
Dod of butter for greasing

I'm scared already ...

1. Ask your Grown-Up to set the oven to 190 °C/Gas Mark 5
2. With the dod of butter on a piece of greaseproof paper grease the baking tray.
3. Weigh out the sugar and soft margarine and put them in the mixing bowl.
4. Add the salt and vanilla drops and mix it all together with your wooden spoon.
5. Weigh the flour and add this to the mixing bowl along with the cocoa and ginger.
6. Bind it all together adding a little milk if it is too stiff. You should now have a doughlike lump.
7. Use you clean hands to lift this from the bowl onto a lightly floured place (the table or work surface.)
8. Knead this with your hands until it is smooth
9. Taking your rolling pin (remember to flour it too) and roll out the dough to about 5mm.
10. Using your scary monster biscuit cutters stamp out up to 16 biscuits.
11. Place them onto the greased tray, pop them in the oven and bake for 10-15 minutes.
12. Cool them on your wire rack before decorating.
13. To make the icing, weigh the icing sugar and put it into the smaller mixing bowl.
14. Using your teaspoon mix it with the hot water (don't overdo the amount) to make lovely icing.
15. You can add colour like red and black using small drops of food colouring. *HAVE A GO ... AGHHHHHHHHH!!!*

Mr Tilly's Tips

Pete the Goldfish's Scary Ginger Biscuits

What do you need to knead?

Cookie dough or bread dough (that is the big gooey lump you get before cooking) needs to be kneaded. This means worked with your hands over and over. It's like wrapping it over itself again and again. This takes a bit of getting used to so ask a Grown-Up to show you (or let them do it if they want to!).

Scary Monster Faces

This is the fun bit.

Design some scary faces before you get busy with the icing.

Whooooo!!!

Heather's Tablet

What you need in the kitchen

30CM X 20CM BAKING TRAY
WEIGHING SCALES
LARGE HEAVY BASED SAUCEPAN
SAUCER
TEASPOON
KNIFE
WOODEN SPOON

Ingredients (what's in it!)

25g salted butter
1 full fat 410g tin evaporated milk
0.9 kg castor sugar
1 teaspoon vanilla essence
Dod of butter

Warning! Warning! Warning!

This is one to only do with a Grown Up because boiling sugar is very very hot and if it splashes you it could leave blisters - so be very careful ...

1. Put the dod of butter on a piece of greaseproof paper and grease your baking tray.
2. Weigh the butter and put it in the saucepan over a very low heat to melt it.
3. Add the tin of evaporated milk.
4. Weigh the sugar and add it too. STIR with your wooden spoon.
5. Now turn the heat up a little and bring the mixture to the boil stirring all the while to prevent it sticking and burning.
6. Keep boiling for 20 minutes or until the mixture sounds sticky (When you rub the back of your wooden spoon back and forth it clicks.) You will also see that the colour has changed and become slightly darker.
7. Test by putting a teaspoon of mixture into a saucer of very cold water. If it starts to set (go hard) it is time to take it off the heat.
8. Add the vanilla essence and beat the mixture hard for five minutes.
9. Pour the HOT mixture into your tray.
10. Leave it to cool in the fridge.
11. Cut into squares and share.

BE CAREFUL NOT TO EAT TOO MUCH
BECAUSE ONCE YOU START IT'S HARD TO STOP.

Mr Tilly's Tips

Heather's Tablet

Is the butter salted or unsalted?
Yes there are two types of butter, SALTED and UNSALTED. Sometimes the recipe doesn't tell you, it simply says butter.

If you aren't sure then use UNSALTED but in Heather's Tablet she wants it SALTED.

Is it set?
When you make tablet or jam you want it to set. This means when it stops being runny and thickens up.

What is the difference between tablet and fudge?
Tablet is a sort of Scottish version of fudge. Fudge is soft and a bit gooey but tablet is harder. Both are delicious and both make good presents. Talking of which ...

Present idea
Find a little box or basket. Line it with scrunched up tissue paper and place your tablet chunks inside. Put a ribbon around it and attach a wee tag. I can think of lots of people in my village who would just love a present like this.

Archie Russell's Treacle Buns

What you need in the kitchen

LARGE MIXING BOWL   WEIGHING SCALES
SIEVE   MICROWAVE PROOF JUG
FORK   FLAT TIN
TABLESPOON   TEASPOON
WIRE RACK   COOKIE CUTTER

Ingredients (what's in it!)

375g self raising flour
Extra flour for dusting
50g margarine
100g castor sugar
1 pinch bicarbonate of soda
Half a teaspoon of baking powder
Large tablespoon treacle
10 fluid ounces luke warm milk
1 egg

Archie has been eating these since he was a wee boy ... that's a lot of buns!

1. Ask a Grown-Up to set the oven to 200 °C/Gas Mark 6.
2. Weigh and sieve the flour into your mixing bowl.
3. Add the bicarbonate of soda and baking powder.
4. Weigh the sugar and margarine and add them too.
5. Using your CLEAN HANDS rub the margarine into the dry ingredients. There is a knack to this which a Grown-Up can show you. It's all about lifting and rubbing everything in the bowl between your fingers and thumbs until you have made something that looks like fine breadcrumbs. Set aside.
6. Measure out your milk in the microwave proof jug and put it in the microwave for one minute.
7. Crack in the egg and pour in the treacle and mix with your fork.
8. Return to your large mixing bowl and make a well in the middle of the flour mixture.
9. Pour the egg/treacle mixture into the well and using your fork mix it all up together. This should not be too sloppy or too dry.
10. Dust a little flour onto a table or board or surface and press the dough down onto it until it is about two thirds of a centimetre thick (you don't need a rolling pin).
11. Using your cookie cutter, cut out the scones. You may get up to 7 scones although this depends on the size of your cookie cutter!

12. Sprinkle a little flour over the flat tin and then place your buns onto it.
13. Bake the buns for about 12/15 minutes.
14. When they are ready lift them onto the wire rack to cool.

ARCHIE SAYS THEY ARE MOST DELICIOUS
WHEN YOU EAT THEM WARM WITH YUMMY BUTTER
AHHHHH ...

Mr Tilly's Tips

Archie Russell's Treacle Buns

Luke warm milk?
There is a boy in our village called Luke who is always playing with a ball. Bridget says if he keeps practising he will play for Scotland. How exciting! If I keep playing with my ball maybe I can play for Scotland too. Anyway I don't think this has anything to do with him.

When you are asked to make something luke warm it means not boiling hot and not cold but somewhere in between.

Halloween Party Fun
The boys in the scouts had a party last Halloween. They all dressed up and played games. What a mess they made and what fun for a dog like me to hoover up afterwards.

Why not have a go at drawing your favourite Halloween outfit.

Daisy's Pumpkin Biscuits

What you need in the kitchen

WEIGHING SCALES   LARGE MIXING BOWL
BAKING TRAY   ROLLING PIN
BISCUIT CUTTER   PASTRY BRUSH
SAUCEPAN   TEASPOON

Ingredients (what's in it!)

200g plain flour
50g brown sugar
2½ teaspoons baking powder
Half a teaspoon salt
Quarter of a teaspoon bicarbonate of soda
100g butter
80g buttermilk
150g mashed cooked pumpkin pureed
Dod of butter
Extra flour for dusting

Ask your Grown-Up to dig out and cook the flesh when you carve your pumpkin ...

1. Now ask them to set the oven to 230 °C/Gas Mark 7.
2. Put a dod of butter onto some greaseproof paper and grease the baking tray.
3. Weigh out your flour and sugar and butter and put them into your large mixing bowl.
4. Add the baking powder, bicarbonate of soda and salt.
5. Rub the butter into the flour with your fingers and thumbs (you might need a Grown-Up to show you how), until the mixture looks like coarse breadcrumbs.
6. Now add the pumpkin puree and buttermilk and bind it all together with your NICE CLEAN HANDS until it forms a dough.
7. Dust the board or table with some flour and turn your dough out onto it.
8. Pat or roll with your floured rolling pin until the dough is an old inch thick.
9. Cut with the biscuit cutter into about 6 biscuits.
10. Place the biscuits about 1 old inch apart on the tray.
11. Bake for 18-22 minutes or until they look golden brown.
12. Take your saucepan and melt a little butter in it over a low heat.
13. When the biscuits come out of the oven brush them with the melted butter using a pastry brush.
14 Eat them warm and scrumptious.

Daisy got this recipe from her Granny and every Halloween they make these in her house for the guisers.

Mr Tilly's Tips

Daisy's Pumpkin Biscuits

Plain or self raising flour?

There are several different types of flour. In this book we mainly use two, PLAIN and SELF RAISING.

PLAIN FLOUR is used for pastry and biscuits and things we do not want to rise or grow. However if we add baking powder and bicarbonate of soda to plain flour they give the biscuits a little rise and spread so that they are more airy and less hard.

SELF RAISING FLOUR is used for cakes to make them puff up and RISE beautifully.

Pureed?

Means all mashed up!

Pumpkin Fun!

Draw some weird and wonderful faces on pumpkins like these to copy when you do the real thing.

YIKES.

Winter

The heavy sky hangs overhead
As I dash through sleeping trees.
The children are wearing hats and gloves
And there's an icy breeze.

Robin's in the garden
As we head up the lane for a sledge.
The snow goes crunch beneath my paws
And hangs from the trees and the hedge.

Let's get to the warmth of the kitchen
Before there is even more snow.
White flakes melt on my nose and ears
And I long for the fire's glow.

Christmas time will cheer us up
Hang your biscuit stars in the tree.
Let's make some Christmas Clusters
And Chocolate Brownies for tea.

Don't forget the Clutie Dumpling
And Cranberry Muffins too.
There are carols on the radio
And surprises and presents for YOU.

Recipes

Bridget's Exceptional Christmas Clusters

Sarah's Star Biscuits

Mr Patel's Orange and Cranberry Muffins

Alison's Mum's Chocolate Brownies

Bridget's Exceptional Christmas Clusters

What you need in the kitchen

MICROWAVABLE BOWL
WOODEN SPOON
SMALL PAPER CASES

LARGE MIXING BOWL
TEASPOON
WEIGHING SCALES

Ingredients (what's in it!)

225g white chocolate
50g sunflower seeds
50g almond flakes
50g sesame seeds
50g seedless raisins
1 teaspoon ground cinnamon

This one is so easy and fun to take to Christmas Parties ...

1. Break the chocolate up and put it into a microwavable bowl. Heat on medium for 3 minutes.
2. Weigh out your other ingredients and put them into a large mixing bowl.
3. Add the melted chocolate and stir well with your wooden spoon.
4. Using your teaspoon, spoon the mixture into the small paper cases.
5. Pop them into the fridge to set.

DON'T YOU JUST LOVE THE SNOW?

Mr Tilly's Tips

Bridget's Exceptional Christmas Clusters

Microwavable bowl?

Did you know that there are some things you cannot put in the microwave?

Pudding basins and plates and mugs?

Plastic things?

Always check with a Grown Up first.

Sarah's Star Biscuits

What you need in the kitchen

TWO BAKING TRAYS
WEIGHING SCALES
ROLLING PIN
WIRE RACK
MIXING BOWL

WOODEN SPOON
SIEVE
STAR SHAPED CUTTER
GRATER
CLING FILM

Ingredients (what's in it!)

175g unsalted butter
300g caster sugar
300g plain flour
1 egg
1 egg yolk
1 teaspoon vanilla essence
Grated rind of 1 lemon
Pinch of salt
Dod of butter

Sarah gives these as presents and hangs them in her Christmas Tree ...

1. Ask a Grown-Up to set the oven to 190 °C/Gas Mark 5.
2. Use your dod of butter on a piece of greaseproof paper to grease two baking trays.
3. Weigh out your butter and put it into the mixing bowl.
4. Beat the butter with your wooden spoon until it's nice and soft. (This takes some strength so if your Grown-Up has a machine let them use it otherwise just keep going strong one).
5. Weigh out your sugar and add it to the butter a little at a time all the while beating with that spoon. The mixture should look light and fluffy.
6. Crack in one egg and ask a Grown-Up to help you separate the yolk from the white on the second egg so that you can have just the yolk for your biscuit. Plop it in and mix mix mix.
7. Add the vanilla essence and salt.
8. Rub your lemon against a grinder over your mixing bowl so that the outside or the rind also goes in. Mix.
9. Weigh out the flour and using a sieve sift it into your mixing bowl. Stir it all in.
10. Now using your **NICE CLEAN HANDS** gather up the dough into a big ball.
11. Wrap it up in cling film and pop it into the fridge for 30 minutes. (This is a good time to wash and tidy up and rest your tired arms after all that mixing).

12. Take the dough from the fridge, unwrap it and put it on a board or work surface which you have sprinkled flour over (you are getting good at dusting!).
13. Roll it out with your flour dusted rolling pin until about 3mm thick.
14. Take your star cutter and cut out about 24 biscuits.
15. Place them on the trays and using something sharp like a skewer or a knife tip make a wee hole at the top of one of the star points (You may need the Grown-Up for this).
    This is so that when they are baked you can put a piece of thread or a ribbon through to hang the biscuits in your tree.
16. Bake for about 8 minutes until lightly coloured. Cool them for a minute before putting them on the wire rack.

THERE ARE STARS EVERYWHERE AND YOU ARE ONE OF THEM.

Mr Tilly's Tips

Sarah's Star Biscuits

Why sieve?
Sieving is fun.
We can catch all the sugary lumps.
We can also make the flour full
of air so that our cakes
and biscuits are delicious and light.

Stars in the Tree
Make sure you make a big enough hole in your stars if you want to put them on the tree. Thread them with ribbon and hang them with the Christmas chocolates.

Stars on a dish
Dust your stars with icing sugar by shaking the sugar through a sieve. It falls like fine snow and makes the biscuits look even more Christmassy.

Stars as a gift
You can give your sugar dusted stars as a gift to someone special at any time of the year.

Mr Patel's Orange and Cranberry Muffins

What you need in the kitchen

WEIGHING SCALES
SMALL MIXING BOWL
TEASPOON
FORK
MUFFIN TIN
GRATER
WIRE RACK

LARGE MIXING BOWL
SIEVE
WOODEN SPOON
CUP
12 MUFFIN CASES
SMALL SAUCEPAN

Ingredients (what's in it!)

180g plain flour
60g caster sugar
2 teaspoons baking powder
2 teaspoons grated orange rind
2 eggs
Quarter teaspoon salt
50g melted butter
175ml milk
175g fresh cranberries

Apart from Mr Patel's amazing curries these are his children's favourites ...

1. Ask a Grown-Up to set the oven to 200 °C/Gas Mark 6.
2. Put the muffin cases in a muffin tin.
3. Weigh out your flour and sugar and sift them into your mixing bowl.
4. Add the salt and set aside.
5. Crack the eggs into your smaller mixing bowl and whisk them with a fork.
6. Melt the butter in your small saucepan. Let it cool.
7. Take the grater and rub an orange to make the rind. Try and make two teaspoons worth and put it into the whisked egg.
8. When the butter is cooler add it to the eggs too along with the milk and stir it all together with your fork.
9. Go back to the large mixing bowl and make a well in the middle of the flour.
10. Pour the egg mix into the well and mix with the wooden spoon.
11. Now add the fresh cranberries and mix them in, but be careful not to crush the cranberries because we want them whole in the muffins.
12. Using your teaspoon, spoon the mixture into the paper cases. Don't fill them too full because they will rise.
13. Bake for 20-25 minutes until the tops spring back when you touch them (this is a Grown-Up's job.)
14. Leave the muffins in the tin for 5 minutes and then put them on a wire rack to cool.

WOWZER!!!

Mr Tilly's Tips

Mr Patel's Orange and Cranberry Muffins

Muffin or a faerie cake?
Which is bigger, a muffin or a faerie cake? Yes you are right, the mighty muffin is bigger by far. So make sure you have the right sized paper cake cases!

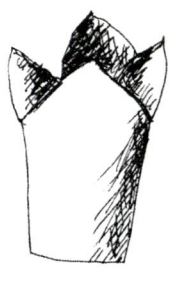

Have a cracking time
You can crack your eggs either by tapping against the side of your mixing bowl or by gently hitting with a dinner knife. Either way it takes practice and don't worry if you have to fish out a few bits of shell until you get good at it.

Whisk it all up
As a beginner cook a fork is good to whisk with. Grown-Ups often use an electric handheld whisk because it's quicker or whisk things together in a food mixer machine.
Let them help out if they want to but for now work on moving the fork quickly through the mixture to make bubbles.

Alison's Mum's Chocolate Brownies

What you need in the kitchen

WEIGHING SCALES
WOODEN SPOON
PENCIL AND SCISSORS
SMALL BAKING TRAY

LARGE MIXING BOWL
TABLESPOON
KNIFE
MICROWAVABLE BOWL

Ingredients (what's in it!)

175g butter
175g self raising flour
350g castor sugar
250g dark chocolate
4 eggs
Tablespoon milk
Greaseproof paper
Dod of butter

These are such a yummy treat on a Winter's day with a nice glass of milk ...

1. Ask your Grown-Up to set the oven to 150 °C/Gas Mark 2/3
2. Using your dod of butter grease the baking tray.
3. Place the tray onto a sheet of greaseproof paper and draw around it.
4. Cut out the shape and put it into the bottom of the baking tray.
5. Break the chocolate into pieces into the microwavable bowl.
6. Weigh the butter and put in the bowl too.
7. Place in the microwave for 2-4 minutes until the chocolate and butter have melted.
8. Crack the eggs into your large mixing bowl.
9. Weigh out your sugar and add it to the eggs along with the milk.
10. Stir together with your wooden spoon.
11. Weigh out and add the flour. Keep mixing.
12. Add the melted chocolate mixture and mix again. In fact beat it well.
13. Bake in the oven for 30-35 minutes. It will be crispy on top and gooey in the middle.
14. Whilst still warm mark into 12 pieces.
15. Allow to cool and eventually put in the fridge.
16. Once cold, cut the pieces out of the tin and enjoy with friends.

THESE ARE FOR SHARING ...

Mr Tilly's Tips

Alison's Mum's Chocolate Brownies

Chocolate and dogs

Did you know that chocolate is bad for dogs? The worst kind is the high cocoa stuff. So no chocolate brownie for me. I must just enjoy the smell and watch other people oohing and ahhing when they have a bite. Life isn't always fair.

Mark out your brownies while they are still hot

They will be a wee bit crumbly when they are warm so don't try to take your brownies out of the tin until they have cooled down. Cut through with a knife and get them out of the tin when they are cool and less likely to fall apart.

Hope you enjoy Baking as much as we enjoyed Making

Lightning Source UK Ltd.
Milton Keynes UK
UKRC02n0003231117
313190UK00005B/79